projects from your SCRAP BAG

If you crochet, you have them. They're clumped together in bags or boxes, or maybe hiding under your bed. They're those inevitable partial-skeins of yarn, the ones that are too good to throw away. But what do you do with them, other than letting them clutter up your life?

How about crocheting a vibrant jacket that goes with absolutely everything? Maybe you need a throw pillow or an afghan with all the zing you've been wishing for. A hodge-podge of fibers can also be crocheted into a terrific wool-acrylic-nylon, etc., tote. So, there's really no good reason for letting those yummy bits of yarn languish with the dust bunnies. Bring them out into the light of day and enjoy creating your own fashions.

The power to empty your scrap bag while enhancing your environment is in your talented fingers.

Leisure Arts, Inc.
Little Rock, AR

coat of many colors

■■■□ INTERMEDIATE

Size: **Finished Chest Measurement:**
Small   41½"   (105.5 cm)
Medium   44"   (112 cm)
Large   48¼"   (122.5 cm)
X-Large   51½"   (131 cm)

Size Note: Instructions are written for size Small, with sizes Medium, Large, and X-Large in braces { }. Instructions will be easier to read if you circle all the numbers pertaining to your size. If only one number is given, it applies to all sizes.

MATERIALS

Medium Weight Yarn [4]
    Assorted Colors - 28{32-36-40} ounces
       [800{910-1,020-1,140} grams] total
    Black - 3½ ounces (100 grams)
Crochet hook, size H (5 mm) **or** size needed
    for gauge
Yarn needle

GAUGE: In pattern,
            13 sts and 10 rows = 4" (10 cm)

Gauge Swatch: 4" (10 cm) square
Ch 14.
Work same as Back for 10 rows; do **not** change colors at end of last row, finish off.

STITCH GUIDE

SINGLE CROCHET DECREASE
 (abbreviated sc decrease)
Pull up a loop in next 2 sts, YO and draw through all 3 loops on hook **(counts as one sc)**.
DOUBLE CROCHET DECREASE
 (abbreviated dc decrease) (uses next 2 sts)
★ YO, insert hook in **next** st, YO and pull up a loop, YO and draw through 2 loops on hook; repeat from ★ once **more**, YO and draw through all 3 loops on hook **(counts as one dc)**.

Note: Change colors at the end of every row **(Fig. 1a, page 18)**, unless otherwise instructed.

BACK

With first color, ch 66{70-76-82}.

Row 1: Sc in second ch from hook and in each ch across: 65{69-75-81} sc.

Row 2 (Right side): Ch 3 **(counts as first dc, now and throughout)**, turn; dc in next sc and in each sc across.

Note: Loop a short piece of yarn around any stitch to mark Row 2 as **right** side.

Row 3: Ch 1, turn; sc in each dc across.

Row 4: Ch 3, turn; dc in next sc and in each sc across.

Rows 5-38: Repeat Rows 3 and 4, 17 times.

Instructions continued on page 4.

ARMHOLE SHAPING

Row 1: Ch 1, turn; slip st in first 5{7-7-9} dc, ch 1, sc in same st and in each dc across to last 4{6-6-8} dc, leave remaining dc unworked: 57{57-63-65} sc.

Rows 2 thru 18{22-22-24}: Repeat Rows 2 and 3, 8{10-10-11} times; then repeat Row 2 once **more**; at end of last row, do **not** change colors, finish off.

RIGHT FRONT
BODY

With first color, ch 36{38-42-44}.

Row 1: Sc in second ch from hook and in each ch across: 35{37-41-43} sc.

Row 2 (Right side): Ch 3, turn; dc in next sc and in each sc across.

Note: Mark Row 2 as **right** side.

Row 3: Ch 1, turn; sc in each dc across.

Row 4: Ch 3, turn; dc in next sc and in each sc across.

Rows 5-38: Repeat Rows 3 and 4, 17 times.

ARMHOLE SHAPING

Row 1: Ch 1, turn; slip st in first 5{7-7-9} dc, ch 1, sc in same dc and in each dc across: 31{31-35-35} sc.

Rows 2 thru 9{13-13-15}: Repeat Rows 2 and 3, 4{6-6-7} times; at end of last row, do **not** change colors, finish off.

NECK SHAPING

Row 1: With **right** side facing, skip first 5 sc and join yarn with slip st in next sc; ch 3, dc decrease, dc in next sc and in each sc across: 25{25-29-29} dc.

Row 2: Ch 1, turn; sc in each dc across to last 3 dc, sc decrease, sc in last dc: 24{24-28-28} sc.

Row 3: Ch 3, turn; dc decrease, dc in next sc and in each sc across: 23{23-27-27} dc.

Rows 4-9: Repeat Rows 2 and 3, 3 times; at end of Row 9, do **not** change colors, finish off: 17{17-21-21} dc.

LEFT FRONT
BODY

Work same as Right Front to Armhole Shaping.

ARMHOLE SHAPING

Row 1: Ch 1, turn; sc in each dc across to last 4{6-6-8} dc, leave remaining dc unworked: 31{31-35-35} sc.

Rows 2 thru 9{13-13-15}: Repeat Rows 2 and 3, 4{6-6-8} times.

NECK SHAPING

Row 1: Ch 3, turn; dc in next sc and in each sc across to last 8 sc, dc decrease, dc in next sc, leave remaining 5 sc unworked: 25{25-29-29} dc.

Row 2: Ch 1, turn; sc in first dc, sc decrease, sc in each dc across: 24{24-28-28} sc.

Row 3: Ch 3, turn; dc in next sc and in each sc across to last 3 sc, dc decrease, dc in last sc: 23{23-27-27} dc.

Rows 4-9: Repeat Rows 2 and 3, 3 times; at end of Row 9, do **not** change colors, finish off: 17{17-21-21} dc.

SLEEVE (Make 2)

With first color, ch 32{32-34-36}.

Row 1: Sc in second ch from hook and in each ch across: 31{31-33-35} sc.

Row 2 (Right side): Ch 3, turn; dc in next sc and in each sc across.

Note: Mark Row 2 as **right** side.

Row 3: Ch 1, turn; sc in each dc across.

Row 4 (Increase row)**:** Ch 3, turn; dc in same st and in each sc across to last sc, 2 dc in last sc: 33{33-35-37} dc.

Rows 5 thru 8{10-16-20}: Repeat Rows 3 and 4, 2{3-6-8} times: 37{39-47-53} dc.

Increase Row: Ch 1, turn; 2 sc in first dc, sc in each dc across to last dc, 2 sc in last dc: 39{41-49-55} sc.

Next 3 rows: Work even.

Repeat last 4 rows, 4{8-4-4} times: 47{57-57-63} sts.

Work even until Sleeve measures 20" (51 cm), at end of last row, do **not** change colors, finish off.

Sew shoulder seams.

COLLAR

Row 1: With **right** side facing, join yarn with sc at Right Neck edge **(see Joining With Sc, page 17)**; work 45 sc evenly spaced across neck edge: 46 sc.

Row 2: Ch 3, turn; dc in next sc and in each sc across.

Row 3: Ch 1, turn; sc in each dc across.

Rows 4-7: Repeat Rows 2 and 3 twice; at end of Row 7, do **not** change colors, finish off.

Sew Sleeves to Body, matching center of last row on Sleeve to shoulder seam and sides of Sleeve to skipped sts at Armhole.

Weave underarm and side in one continuous seam **(Fig. 4, page 18)**.

BODY TRIM

With **right** side facing, join Black with sc in end of Row 38 on Left Front; working in end of rows, sc evenly across; working in free loops of beginning ch **(Fig. 3, page 18)**, 3 sc in first ch, sc in each ch across to last ch, 3 sc in last ch (corner of Right Front); working in end of rows, sc evenly across to Row 38 of Right Front; finish off.

COLLAR AND LAPEL TRIM

With **wrong** side facing, join Black with slip st in first sc of Body Trim; working in end of rows, sc evenly across; working in unworked sts on Neck Shaping, 3 sc in first sc, sc in each sc across to Collar; sc evenly spaced across end of rows on Collar; working across last row of Collar, 3 sc in first sc, sc in each sc across to last sc, 3 sc in last sc; sc evenly spaced across end of rows on Collar; working in unworked sts on Neck Shaping, sc in each st across to last st, 3 sc in last st; working in end of rows on Right Front, sc evenly across; join with slip st to last sc of Body Trim, finish off.

SLEEVE TRIM

With **right** side facing and working in free loops of beginning ch, join Black with sc in any ch; sc in each ch around; join with slip st to first sc, finish off.

Repeat for second Sleeve.

expressions of color

●■□□ EASY

Finished Pillow Size: 15" (38 cm) long

MATERIALS

Medium Weight Yarn
   Assorted Colors - 8 ounces (230 grams) total
Crochet hook, size I (5.5 mm) **or** size needed
   for gauge
Polyester fiberfill
Yarn needle

GAUGE: 13 hdc and 9 rnds = 4" (10 cm)

Gauge Swatch: 4" (10 cm) square
Ch 14.
Row 1: Hdc in third ch from hook **(2 skipped chs count as first hdc)**, hdc in next ch and in each ch across: 13 hdc.
Rows 2-9: Ch 2 **(counts as first hdc)**, turn; hdc in next hdc and in each hdc across.
Finish off.

Note: Each round is worked in a different color.

END (Make 2)
Rnd 1: With first color, ch 3, 9 hdc in third ch from hook **(2 skipped chs count as first hdc)**; join with slip st to first hdc; finish off: 10 hdc.

Note: Loop a short piece of yarn around any stitch to mark Rnd 1 as **right** side.

Rnd 2: With **right** side facing, join next color with hdc in any hdc *(see Joining With Hdc, page 18)*; hdc in same st, 2 hdc in next hdc and in each hdc around; join with slip st to first hdc, finish off: 20 hdc.

Rnd 3: With **right** side facing, join next color with hdc in any hdc; 2 hdc in next hdc, (hdc in next hdc, 2 hdc in next hdc) around; join with slip st to first hdc, finish off: 30 hdc.

Rnd 4: With **right** side facing, join next color with hdc in any hdc; hdc in next hdc, 2 hdc in next hdc, (hdc in next 2 hdc, 2 hdc in next hdc) around; join with slip st to first hdc, finish off: 40 hdc.

Rnd 5: With **right** side facing, join next color with hdc in any hdc; hdc in next 2 hdc, 2 hdc in next hdc, (hdc in next 3 hdc, 2 hdc in next hdc) around; join with slip st to first hdc, finish off: 50 hdc.

Rnd 6: With **right** side facing, join next color with hdc in any hdc; hdc in next 3 hdc, 2 hdc in next hdc, (hdc in next 4 hdc, 2 hdc in next hdc) around; join with slip st to first hdc, finish off: 60 hdc.

Rnd 7: With **right** side facing, join next color with hdc in any hdc; hdc in next 4 hdc, 2 hdc in next hdc, (hdc in next 5 hdc, 2 hdc in next hdc) around; join with slip st to first hdc, finish off: 70 hdc.

SIDES
Rnd 1: With **right** side of one End facing and working in Back Loops Only *(Fig. 2, page 18)*, join next color with hdc in any hdc; hdc in next hdc and in each hdc around; join with slip st to **both** loops of first hdc, finish off.

Rnd 2: With **right** side facing and working in **both** loops, join next color with hdc in any hdc; hdc in next hdc and in each hdc around; join with slip st to first hdc, finish off.

Repeat Rnd 2 until Sides measure approximately 15" (38 cm).

Stuff Pillow firmly.

With **wrong** sides together, matching sts and working through **inside** loops only, whipstitch second End to last rnd of Sides *(Fig. 5, page 19)*.

kaleidoscope

Finished Pillow Size: 16" (40.5 cm) square

MATERIALS

Medium Weight Yarn
   Assorted Colors - 8 ounces (230 grams) total
Crochet hook, size H (5 mm) **or** size needed for
   gauge
Polyester fiberfill

GAUGE: 15 hdc = 4" (10 cm)

Gauge Swatch: 4¹/₂" (11.5 cm)
Work same as Center through Rnd 5.

STITCH GUIDE

> **HALF DOUBLE CROCHET DECREASE**
> *(abbreviated hdc decrease)*
> (uses next 2 hdc)
> ★ YO, insert hook in **next** hdc, YO and pull up
> a loop; repeat from ★ once **more**, YO and draw
> through all 5 loops on hook **(counts as one
> hdc)**.

Note: Each round is worked in a different color.

SQUARE (Make 2)
CENTER

With any color, ch 4; join with slip st to form a ring.

Rnd 1 (Right side)**:** Ch 2 **(counts as first hdc)**,
15 hdc in ring, join with slip st to first hdc;
finish off: 16 hdc.

Note: Loop a short piece of yarn around any stitch
to mark Rnd 1 as **right** side.

Rnd 2: With **right** side facing, join next color with
hdc in any hdc **(see *Joining With Hdc, page 18)*;
4 hdc in same st, skip next hdc, hdc in next hdc,
skip next hdc, ★ 5 hdc in next hdc, skip next hdc,
hdc in next hdc, skip next hdc; repeat from ★
2 times **more**, join with slip st to first hdc; finish off:
24 hdc.

Rnds 3-13: With **right** side facing, join next color
with hdc in center hdc of any corner 5-hdc group;
4 hdc in same st, skip next hdc, hdc in next hdc and
in each hdc across to next corner hdc, ★ 5 hdc in
next hdc, skip next hdc, hdc in each hdc across to
next corner hdc; repeat from ★ 2 times **more**; join
with slip st to first hdc, finish off: 156 hdc.

CORNER

Row 1: With **right** side facing, join next color with
hdc in fourth hdc of any corner 5-hdc group; skip
next hdc, hdc decrease, hdc in next hdc and in
each hdc across to within one hdc of next corner
hdc, skip next hdc, hdc in corner hdc, leave
remaining sts unworked; finish off: 36 hdc.

Rows 2-11: With **right** side facing, join next color
with hdc in first hdc; skip next hdc, hdc decrease,
hdc in next hdc and in each hdc across to last
2 hdc, skip next hdc, hdc in last hdc; finish off:
6 hdc.

Repeat for remaining 3 corners.

EDGING

With **wrong** side facing, join next color with sc in any hdc *(see Joining With Sc, page 17)*; sc evenly around entire Square working in each st and in end of rows; join with slip st to first sc, finish off.

FINISHING

With **wrong** sides together and working through **both** loops on both pieces, join next color with sc in any st on Edging; sc evenly around 3 sides. Stuff firmly, sc across last side; join with slip st to first sc, finish off.

rainbow stripes

◼◼◻◻ EASY

Finished Tote Size: 12"h x 19"w (30.5 cm x 48.5 cm), excluding handles

MATERIALS

Medium Weight Yarn
  Black - 8 ounces
  Assorted colors - 8 ounces (230 grams) total
Crochet hook, size K (6.5 mm) **or** size needed
  for gauge
Yarn needle

GAUGE: 11 sc and 10 rnds = 4" (10 cm)

Gauge Swatch: 4" (10 cm) square
With two strands of yarn held together, ch 12.
Row 1: Sc in second ch from hook and in each ch across.
Rows 2-10: Ch 1, turn; sc in each sc across.
Finish off.

Note: Tote is made holding one strand of Black and one strand of Scrap Color together throughout. Change Scrap Color as desired *(Figs. 1a & b, page 18)*.

TOTE
BOTTOM
With one strand of Black and one strand of Scrap Color held together, ch 27.

Rnd 1 (Right side)**:** Sc in second ch from hook and in each ch across to last ch, 3 sc in last ch; working in free loops of beginning ch *(Fig. 3, page 18)*, sc in next 24 chs, 2 sc in same ch as first sc; join with slip st to first sc: 54 sc.

Note: Loop a short piece of yarn around any stitch to mark Rnd 1 as **right** side.

Rnd 2: Ch 1, 2 sc in same st, sc in next 24 sc, 2 sc in each of next 3 sc, sc in next 24 sc, 2 sc in each of last 2 sc; join with slip st to first sc: 60 sc.

Rnd 3: Ch 1, sc in same st, 2 sc in next sc, sc in next 24 sc, 2 sc in next sc, (sc in next sc, 2 sc in next sc) twice, sc in next 25 sc, (2 sc in next sc, sc in next sc) twice; join with slip st to first sc: 66 sc.

Rnd 4: Ch 1, 2 sc in same st, sc in next 26 sc, 2 sc in next sc, (sc in next 2 sc, 2 sc in next sc) twice, sc in next 26 sc, (2 sc in next sc, sc in next 2 sc) twice; join with slip st to first sc: 72 sc.

Rnd 5: Ch 1, sc in same st, 2 sc in next sc, sc in next 25 sc, 2 sc in next sc, (sc in next 4 sc, 2 sc in next sc) twice, sc in next 25 sc, 2 sc in next sc, sc in next 4 sc, 2 sc in next sc, sc in last 3 sc; join with slip st to first sc: 78 sc.

Rnd 6: Ch 1, sc in same st and in next sc, 2 sc in next sc, sc in next 26 sc, 2 sc in next sc, (sc in next 5 sc, 2 sc in next sc) twice, sc in next 26 sc, 2 sc in next sc, sc in next 5 sc, 2 sc in next sc, sc in last 3 sc; join with slip st to first sc: 84 sc.

Rnd 7: Ch 1, sc in same st and in next 2 sc, 2 sc in next sc, sc in next 27 sc, 2 sc in next sc, (sc in next 6 sc, 2 sc in next sc) twice, sc in next 27 sc, 2 sc in next sc, sc in next 6 sc, 2 sc in next sc, sc in last 3 sc; join with slip st to first sc: 90 sc.

Rnd 8: Ch 1, sc in same st and in next sc, 2 sc in next sc, sc in next 30 sc, 2 sc in next sc, (sc in next 6 sc, 2 sc in next sc) twice, sc in next 30 sc, 2 sc in next sc, sc in next 6 sc, 2 sc in next sc, sc in last 4 sc; join with slip st to first sc: 96 sc.

BODY

Rnd 1: Ch 1, working in Back Loops Only *(Fig. 2, page 18)*, sc in same st and in each sc around, do **not** join, place a marker *(see Markers, page 18)*.

Rnd 2: Working in **both** loops, sc in each sc around.

Repeat Rnd 2 until Body measures 12" (30.5 cm) **or** to desired height; at end of last rnd, slip st in next sc, finish off.

Instructions continued on page 16.

odds 'n ends

Finished Afghan Size: 40¹/₂" x 48¹/₂"
(103 cm x 123 cm)

Note: Finished size of the Afghan can be varied by making a beginning ch of any length and working Afghan to desired length, adjusting yarn amount accordingly.

MATERIALS

MEDIUM 4

Medium Weight Yarn
Assorted colors - 26 ounces (740 grams) total
Crochet hook, size K (6.5 mm) **or** size needed for gauge

GAUGE: In pattern,
11 sts and 8 rows = 4" (10 cm)

Gauge Swatch: 4" (10 cm) square
Ch 13.
Work same as Afghan for 8 rows.
Finish off.

Note: To make a "raggy ball," cut scrap yarn into 36" (91.5 cm) lengths. This can be done quickly by holding several strands together, wrapping them around a book or piece of cardboard, then cut yarn at the bottom (as though you are making fringe). Tie random strands together with one overhand knot leaving random length ends; do **not** trim ends. Wind in a ball as you go. When you have a ball about the size of a melon, begin Afghan. If you run out of raggy ball, tie on new lengths as needed while working. Keep ties to **right** side.

AFGHAN

Ch 116, place marker in fourth ch from hook for st placement.

Row 1 (Right side)**:** Dc in fourth ch from hook and in each ch across **(3 skipped chs count as first dc):** 114 dc.

Note: Loop a short piece of yarn around any stitch to mark Row 1 as **right** side.

Row 2: Ch 2 **(counts as first hdc)**, turn; hdc in next dc and in each dc across.

Row 3: Ch 3 **(counts as first dc)**, turn; dc in next hdc and in each hdc across.

Repeat Rows 2 and 3 until Afghan measures approximately 48" (122 cm), ending by working Row 3, do **not** finish off.

EDGING

Ch 1, turn; 3 sc in first dc, sc in each dc across to last dc, 3 sc in last dc; sc evenly spaced across end of rows to marked ch; working in free loops of beginning ch *(Fig. 3, page 18)*, 3 sc in marked ch, sc in each ch across to last ch, 3 sc in last ch; sc evenly spaced across end of rows; join with slip st to first sc, finish off.

FINISHING

Holding two strands of yarn, each 3" (7.5 cm) long, add fringe evenly around entire Afghan *(Figs. 6a-d, page 19)*.

rainbow squares

rainbow squares

■■■□ INTERMEDIATE

Finished Throw Size: 40" x 46½"
(101.5 cm x 118 cm)

MATERIALS

Medium Weight Yarn
Assorted Colors - 18 ounces (510 grams) total
Black - 6½ ounces (185 grams)
Crochet hook, size H (5 mm) **or** size needed
for gauge

GAUGE: Each Square = 6½" (16.5 cm)

Gauge Swatch: 5½" (14 cm) square
Work same as First Square through Row 12.

Note: Change colors as desired throughout each
Square *(Figs. 1a & b, page 18)*.

FIRST SQUARE
With first color, ch 20.

Row 1 (Right side)**:** Hdc in third ch from hook and
in each ch across **(2 skipped chs count as first hdc):**
19 hdc.

Note: Loop a short piece of yarn around any stitch
to mark Row 1 as **right** side.

Rows 2-12: Ch 2 **(counts as first hdc)**, turn; hdc in
next hdc and in each hdc across.

Finish off.

BORDER
Rnd 1: With **right** side facing, join yarn with sc
in first hdc *(see Joining With Sc, page 17)*, 2 sc
in same hdc, work 18 sc evenly spaced across
to last hdc, 3 sc in last hdc; work 18 sc evenly
spaced across end of rows; working in free loops of
beginning ch *(Fig. 3, page 18)*, 3 sc in first ch, work
18 sc evenly spaced across to last ch, 3 sc in last ch;
work 18 sc evenly spaced across end of rows; join
with slip st to first sc, finish off: 84 sc.

Rnd 2: With **right** side facing, join Black with sc in
center sc of any corner 3-sc group, ch 3, sc in same
st, ★ (ch 3, skip next 2 sc, sc in next sc) 7 times,
ch 3, sc in same sc; repeat from ★ 2 times **more**,
(ch 3, skip next 2 sc, sc in next sc) 6 times, ch 3;
join with slip st to first sc, finish off: 32 ch-3 sps.

ADDITIONAL 41 SQUARES
Work same as First Square through Rnd 1 of Border.

Rnd 2 (Joining rnd)**:** Work One or Two Side Joining
forming 6 vertical strips of 7 Squares each and
arranging Squares as shown in Placement Diagram,
page 16.

ONE SIDE JOINING
Rnd 2 (Joining rnd)**:** With **right** side facing, join
Black with sc in center sc of indicated corner
3-sc group; ★ † (ch 3, skip next 2 sc, sc in next sc)
7 times †, ch 3, sc in same st; repeat from ★ once
more, then repeat from † to † once, ch 1, sc in
corresponding corner ch-3 sp on **previous Square**,
ch 1, sc in same st on **new Square**, (ch 1, sc in next
ch-3 sp on **previous Square**, ch 1, skip next 2 sc on
new Square, sc in next sc) 7 times, ch 1, sc in next
corner ch-3 sp on **previous Square**, ch 1; join with
slip st to first sc, finish off.

Instructions continued on page 16.

TWO SIDE JOINING

Rnd 2 (Joining rnd)**:** With **right** side facing, join Black with sc in center sc of indicated corner 3-sc group; (ch 3, skip next 2 sc, sc in next sc) 7 times, ch 3, sc in same st, (ch 3, skip next 2 sc, sc in next sc) 7 times, ★ ch 1, sc in corresponding corner ch-3 sp on **previous Square**, ch 1, sc in same st on **new Square**, (ch 1, sc in next ch-3 sp on **previous Square**, ch 1, skip next 2 sc on **new Square**, sc in next sc) 7 times; repeat from ★ once **more**, ch 1, sc in next corner ch-3 sp on **previous Square**, ch 1; join with slip st to first sc, finish off.

EDGING

With **right** side facing, join Black with sc in any corner ch-3 sp; ch 3, ★ † (sc in next ch-3 sp or joining, ch 3) across to next corner ch-3 sp †, (sc, ch 3) twice in corner ch-3 sp; repeat from ★ 2 times **more**, then repeat from † to † once, sc in same sp as first sc, ch 3; join with slip st to first sc, finish off.

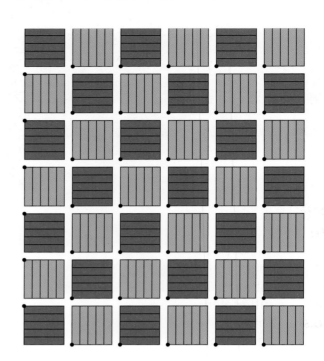

tote

Instructions continued from page 11.

HANDLES

Rnd 1: With **right** side facing, flatten Tote (rounded ends of Bottom should be at the side) and locate the center sc on the last rnd, skip next 9 sc and join yarn with sc in next sc *(see Joining With Sc, page 17)*; sc in next 28 sc, ch 55, skip next 19 sc, sc in next 29 sc, ch 55, leave remaining sts unworked; join with slip st to first sc.

Rnd 2: Ch 1, sc in same st and in each sc and in each ch around; join with slip st to first sc.

Rnd 3: Turn; skip joining slip st, slip st in next sc and in each sc around; join with slip st to first slip st, finish off.

FINISHING

With **wrong** side facing, join next color with slip st in any skipped sc under Handle, slip st in next sc and in each sc and in free loops of each ch around Handle opening; join with slip st to first slip st, finish off.

Repeat for second Handle opening.

general instructions

ABBREVIATIONS

ch(s)	chain(s)
cm	centimeters
dc	double crochet(s)
hdc	half double crochet(s)
mm	millimeters
Rnd(s)	Round(s)
sc	single crochet(s)
sp(s)	space(s)
st(s)	stitch(es)
YO	yarn over

★ — work instructions following ★ as **many more** times as indicated in addition to the first time.

† to † — work all instructions from first † to second † **as many** times as specified.

( ) or [ ] — work enclosed instructions **as many** times as specified by the number immediately following **or** work all enclosed instructions in the stitch or space indicated **or** contains explanatory remarks.

colon (:) — the number(s) given after a colon at the end of a row or round denote(s) the number of stitches you should have on that row or round.

work even — work without increasing or decreasing in the established pattern.

GAUGE

Exact gauge is **essential** for proper size. Before beginning your project, make the sample swatch given in the individual instructions in the yarn and hook specified. After completing the swatch, measure it, counting your stitches and rows carefully. If your swatch is larger or smaller than specified, **make another, changing hook size to get the correct gauge**. Keep trying until you find the size hook that will give you the specified gauge.

JOINING WITH SC

When instructed to join with sc, begin with a slip knot on hook. Insert hook in stitch or space indicated, YO and pull up a loop, YO and draw through both loops on hook.

CROCHET TERMINOLOGY	
UNITED STATES	**INTERNATIONAL**
slip stitch (slip st) =	single crochet (sc)
single crochet (sc) =	double crochet (dc)
half double crochet (hdc) =	half treble crochet (htr)
double crochet (dc) =	treble crochet (tr)
treble crochet (tr) =	double treble crochet (dtr)
double treble crochet (dtr) =	triple treble crochet (ttr)
triple treble crochet (tr tr) =	quadruple treble crochet (qtr)
skip =	miss

CROCHET HOOKS													
U.S.	B-1	C-2	D-3	E-4	F-5	G-6	H-8	I-9	J-10	K-10½	N	P	Q
Metric - mm	2.25	2.75	3.25	3.5	3.75	4	5	5.5	6	6.5	9	10	15

◼◻◻◻ BEGINNER	Projects for first-time crocheters using basic stitches. Minimal shaping.
◼◼◻◻ EASY	Projects using yarn with basic stitches, repetitive stitch patterns, simple color changes, and simple shaping and finishing.
◼◼◼◻ INTERMEDIATE	Projects using a variety of techniques, such as basic lace patterns or color patterns, mid-level shaping and finishing.
◼◼◼◼ EXPERIENCED	Projects with intricate stitch patterns, techniques and dimension, such as non-repeating patterns, multi-color techniques, fine threads, small hooks, detailed shaping and refined finishing.

JOINING WITH HDC

When instructed to join with hdc, begin with a slip knot on hook. YO, holding loop on hook, insert hook in stitch or space indicated, YO and pull up a loop (3 loops on hook), YO and draw through all 3 loops on hook.

MARKERS

Markers are used to help distinguish the beginning of each round being worked. Place a 2" (5 cm) scrap piece of yarn before the first stitch of each round, moving marker after each round is complete.

CHANGING COLORS

Work the last stitch to within one step of completion, hook new yarn and draw through all loops on hook. Cut old yarn.

Fig. 1a   **Fig. 1b**

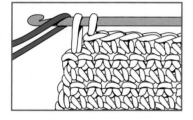   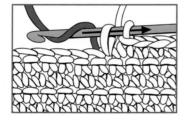

BACK LOOP ONLY

Work only in loop(s) indicated by arrow *(Fig. 2)*.

Fig. 2

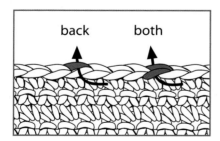

FREE LOOPS OF A CHAIN

When instructed to work in free loops of a chain, work in loop indicated by arrow *(Fig. 3)*.

Fig. 3

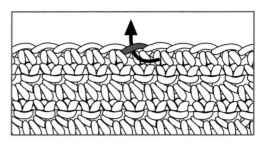

WEAVING

With **wrong** sides together, sew through both pieces once to secure the beginning of the seam, leaving an ample yarn end to weave in later. Insert the needle from **right** to **left** through one strand on each piece *(Fig. 4)*. Bring the needle around and insert it from **right** to **left** through the next strand on both pieces.
Repeat along the edge, being careful to match stitches and rows.

Fig. 4

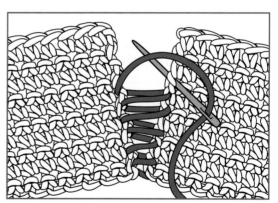

WHIPSTITCH

Place pieces with **wrong** sides together. Beginning in any stitch, sew through both pieces once to secure the beginning of the seam, leaving an ample yarn end to weave in later. Insert the needle from **front** to **back** through **inside** loops only of each stitch on both pieces *(Fig. 5)*. Bring the needle around and insert it from **front** to **back** through next loops of both pieces. Continue in this manner around piece, keeping the sewing yarn fairly loose.

Fig. 5

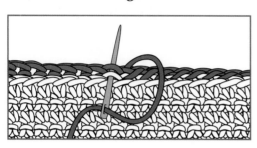

FRINGE

Cut a piece of cardboard 3" (7.5 cm) square. Wind the yarn **loosely** and **evenly** around the cardboard until the card is filled, then cut across one end; repeat as needed.
Hold together two strands of yarn; fold in half. With **wrong** side facing and using a crochet hook, draw the folded end up through a stitch or row and pull the loose ends through the folded end *(Figs. 6a & c)*; draw the knot up **tightly** *(Figs. 6b & d)*. Repeat, spacing as desired.
Lay flat on a hard surface and trim the ends.

Fig. 6a

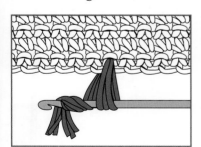

Fig. 6b

Fig. 6c

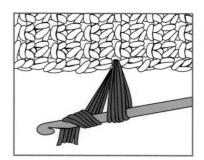

Fig. 6d

YARN INFORMATION

Projects in this leaflet were made using various brands of Medium Weight Yarn. Any brand of Medium Weight Yarn may be used. Remember, to arrive at the finished size, it is the GAUGE/TENSION that is important, not the brand of yarn.

PRODUCTION TEAM:

Instructional Editor - Katie Galucki
Technical Editor - Lois J. Long
Editorial Writer - Susan McManus Johnson
Graphic Artists - Amy Gerke and Jeanne Zaffarano
Senior Graphic Artist - Lora Puls
Photo Stylist - Jessica Wurst
Photographer - Jason Masters

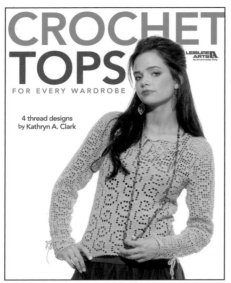

Item # 4089

Item # 4099

Item # 4254

Visit your favorite retailer, or shop online at **leisurearts.com**.

For more inspiration sign up for our free e-newsletter and receive free

projects, reviews of our newest books, handy tips and more. Have questions?

Call us at 1.800.526.5111.

Item # 3888

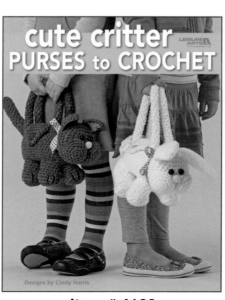

Item # 4160

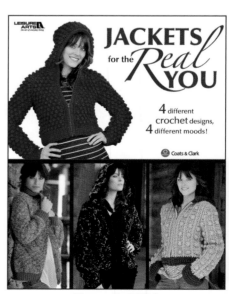

Item # 4261